THE MARINE AQUARIUM

by Richard F. Stratton

yearBOOK

yearBOOKS,INC.
Dr. Herbert R. Axelrod,
Founder & Chairman

Neal Pronek
Chief Editor
Dr. Warren E. Burgess
Editor

yearBOOKS are all photo composed, color separated and designed on Scitex equipment in Neptune, N.J. with the following staff:

COMPUTER ART
  Michael L. Secord
    Supervisor
  Sherise Buhagiar
  Patti Escabi
  Cynthia Fleureton
  Sandra Taylor Gale
  Pat Marotta
  Joanne Muzyka
  Robert Onyrscuk
  Tom Roberts

Advertising Sales
George Campbell
  Chief
Amy Manning
  Coordinator

©yearBOOKS,Inc.
1 TFH Plaza
Neptune, N.J.07753
Completely manufactured in
Neptune, N.J. • USA

Exciting, beautiful, and thoroughly enjoyable, the keeping of marine fishes is a hobby on the rise for people both young and old. Marine fishes are appealing because they allow people to be at peace with themselves in their own living room while watching their fishes in a breathtaking aquarium. Many species can now be kept in the home and further advancements have enabled aquarists to keep their fishes healthier and longer. With a little creativity and the devotion of some time to the keeping of fishes, you will surely develop a great deal of interest in maintaining your own marine aquarium.

In the following pages science teacher Richard F. Stratton provides the reader with information on all phases of the marine aquarium hobby. Those who are thinking about beginning a marine aquarium for the first time, perhaps expanding their current aquarium, or are simply looking for more information, will surely benefit from this yearBOOK.

What are YearBOOKs?

Because keeping Marine Aquarium as a hobby is growing at a rapid pace, information on setting up an aquarium and selecting the right fish for it is vitally needed. Books, the usual way information of this sort is transmitted, can be too slow. Sometimes by the time a book is written and published, the material contained therein is a year or two old...and no new material has been added during that time. Only a book in a magazine form can bring breaking stories and current information. A magazine is streamlined in production, so we have adopted certain magazine publishing techniques in the creation of this yearBOOK. Magazines also can be much cheaper than books because they are supported by advertising. To combine these assets into a great publication, we issued this yearBOOK in both magazine and book format at different prices.

CONTENTS

Balistoides conspicillum

Amphiprion ocellaris

Pomacanthus paru

Gramma loreto

Neocirrhites armatus

THE FISH-ONLY TANK

it would be wise to become proficient with a tank containing only fishes before tackling the living reef system. If you are more interested in invertebrates, then you

Although the sight of a living reef tank can tempt a hobbyist into jumping into such an endeavor with both feet, a little discretion is in order here, as the living reef tank is the most difficult and tricky to handle. Therefore, if your interest is primarily in fishes,

Miniature reef tanks like these are exciting and beautiful — but very difficult! It is best to first become proficient with fish-only tanks, then tackle the reef tanks. Photos courtesy J. P. Burleson, Inc.

Fish-only tanks have as their main priority the display and well-being of the fishes. Decorations may be bleached coral skeletons or artificial coral. Photo by Dr. Herbert R. Axelrod.

could tackle an invertebrate-only tank first, but I am referring here to the non-photosynthetic type of invertebrates. Corals and some anemones are in the more difficult category and need special lighting.   One reason a fish-only tank is easier to begin with is that it leaves out the complication of invertebrates. The fact is that fishes can be quite difficult on invertebrates, for many of them are their natural prey, and, even if they are not, fishes tend to "sample" invertebrates—just out of curiosity if nothing else!

Just to reveal my own natural bias, my first love was fishes, and I still retain an intense interest in them. I became interested in invertebrates primarily as a concommitant of fishes. The fact is that I became sufficiently interested in invertebrates to set up a tank for them only and later graduated to a living reef tank.

Perhaps a few definitions are in order here. A fish-only tank is one in which the main priority is to display and care for fishes. The decorations for such a tank serve also as hiding places for the fishes and may consist of dyed coral skeletons or artificial coral. The advantages of such a tank, besides the fact that we don't have to worry about the fishes harming the invertebrates (or vice versa in certain situations) is that we don't have to worry about special lighting for the photosynthetic invertebrates, and, if there comes a time that there is a need to medicate the fishes, it won't automatically be imperative to remove the fishes to a special hospital tank, as they can be medicated in the main tank without fear of harming the invertebrates, which are generally much more sensitive to medications than the fishes.

Also, certain invertebrates are quite sensitive to water quality, but their metabolism is generally so low that a plethora of invertebrates won't have the same impact on the water as just a few fishes, with their higher metabolic rate. Fishes, on the other hand, have mechanisms for coping with change **as long as it occurs slowly.** My intention, however, is to prevent change as much as possible, and I recommend the following methods for maintaining a fish-only tank.

BASIC FILTRATION

I am a strong advocate of keeping things simple,

Filters are an essential ingredient in keeping the fish-only tanks clean and healthy. Proper filtration can be advantageously combined with periodic water changes for best results. Photo by Guy van den Bossche.

and I have noticed that the freshwater hobbyists who keep either a fish room or a fish house with a multitude of tanks employ only mechanical filters. Usually, these are of the inside variety, and they are driven with air. But, what of the biological filtration? In this case it is irrelevant, as nearly all of these hobbyists make copious use of water changes. Some of them change as much as 50% of the water per day. That keeps metabolites (waste products) from building up, and the inside filters supply aeration and mechanical filtration. (They are, by the way, faithfully changed so that organic debris does not build up to contaminate the water.) Now, can the marine hobbyist employ such a simple system? Yes, but the price would be to have to change up to 50% of the water a day! (Incidentally, most of the hobbyists with fish rooms also keep their tanks clear of gravel unless the fishes need gravel or sand for spawning, as that makes for easy siphoning and helps keep the tank that much more free of organic debris.) Although salt mixes have gotten less expensive, I don't think that many of us are willing to change that much water that often. But it is worthwhile to keep in mind that this basic maintenance system would work if we were willing to pay the price, that is, if we were willing to make daily water changes and frequently clean our little mechanical filters.

A significant step in enhancing success is in the analysis and understanding of the nitrogen cycle. Let us review that now.

THE NITROGEN CYCLE

This concept is discussed with monotonous regularity in nearly all modern books on freshwater and marine aquarium fishes, but, if we go back only two or three decades, we find that even the most thorough of books did not even mention it. That was not because the cycle was not known in science; it was just that it had never been applied to aquarium husbandry, for there had never been a true appreciation of its importance.

Simply put, the nitrogen cycle involves the breaking down of nitrogen-bearing organic compounds into simpler substances. This is done by specific bacteria. The fishes's metabolic processes and the decay of uneaten foods first of all produces quantities of ammonia, which is quite harmful to fishes and many other organisms. Fortunately, there are specific bacteria that break the ammonia down to nitrites, although this is still dangerous to fishes. But then the nitrites are broken down by yet another bacteria into nitrates, which are more easily tolerated than the other two substances. Algae and plants in the aquarium utilize the nitrates in their metabolic processes; however, this is not done in a fast enough manner that the nitrate levels can be ignored, so they should be carefully monitored.

Chemi-Pure removes ammonia and other harmful nitrogenous waste products. Photo courtesy Boyd Enterprises.

All the filtration methods, then, are aimed at the elimination of metabolic compounds from the environment. Thus, mechanical and chemical filtration removes organic matter from the water before it can break down into harmful metabolic compounds. Naturally,

these filters can't do their job unless they are maintained carefully and changed frequently. Biological filters are filters, such as subsand filters or trickle filters or canister filters with media for bacteria in them, that rely upon the action of bacteria to break down the organic compounds into simpler and less harmful products.

MY FAVORITE SYSTEM FOR THE FISH-ONLY TANK

Although I am a technophile of sorts, I am also a great fan of simplicity and reliability. If we went with the simplest system, we would utilize the good old undergravel filter. The only problem is that with the regular undergravel filter there is a tendency to accumulate quite a bit of debris in the water, as it is functioning both as a mechanical filter and a biological filter. That is one of the beauties of it, though. It can do the entire job all by itself. It is, indeed, an efficient filter that is often sold short. Nevertheless, if you utilize it in the normal manner, you will have to siphon out some of the gravel and clean it on a weekly basis to be safe. Not only that, but you should be careful to only siphon out half the gravel in the tank, at the very most, as you don't want to eliminate all of the bacteria that break down the

ammonia and nitrites.

To be sure, there are other options. You can stir the gravel while running a diatom filter. The debris in the tank will be removed from suspension by the filter. As a matter of fact, a diatom filter is a good "ace in the hole" to have on hand. Whenever the water is cloudy from particulate matter or the sand needs cleaning the device can be used. Naturally, it is important that you clean the diatom filter each time it is used. As a matter of fact, it may be necessary to clean the filter several times during a single use. The filter element has such small openings that it can become coated and clogged by the natural slime of the fish that has been sloughed off into the water. Having two or three extra elements is advantageous, and you can later clean them all together by soaking them in a weak solution of bleach. Then be sure to soak them carefully in fresh water that has been treated with a dechlorinator and allow them to dry for several days.

Another strategy is to siphon the tank once a week, and when you do that, utilize one of the vacuuming adapters on your siphon hose. It would be a good idea to make a partial water change of about 10% of your volume once a week. If you want

Regularly scheduled maintenance will be the secret of your success as a marine aquarist. This includes cleaning filters, water changes, and constant checks of the physical properties of the water. Photo by Guy van den Bossche.

to keep your gravel especially clean, you could utilize one of the pump driven vacuum devices. Marine aquarists are gadget lovers by nature, and keeping your gravel clean is an important factor in keeping your tank free from trouble.

A marine tank with an undergravel filter is marine fish keeping at its simplest. You have the sand as a biological filter and as a mechanical filter. It will keep your water clear of debris, and with weekly partial water changes your water should stay clear and not turn yellow. If you live in an area that is subject to smog, you will want to also have a chemical filter of activated carbon. (There are many types of activated carbon, but the type that is best used for marine filtration should be supplied by reputable marine tank commodity specialists.) This can be placed in a canister filter or an outside hang-on type of filter. The carbon should be changed every six months, and don't be afraid to change it even more often if conditions seem to warrant it. Regular maintenance will be the secret to your success as a marine aquarist. If the mechanical and chemical (in the case of the activated carbon) filter is not cleaned regularly, you are not eliminating the organic matter from your aquarium. This is an important fact to keep in mind, as there is no sense in living in a fool's paradise when there is trouble brewing.

There are various ways to improve upon this simple system. Remember that an important part of keeping a marine aquarium is to maintain the pH at a constant level. One way to do that is to keep the bacterial count

To provide additional surfaces on which the beneficial bacteria can grow, many companies have developed artificial filter media with large surface areas for that purpose. Photo courtesy Hagen.

down. There are several ways to do that. One is indirect. If you keep the metabolic content of the water down, there won't be much for the bacteria to subsist upon. (Keep in mind, of course, that we want to foster certain types of bacteria, such as the denitrifying types that help cycle our tank. That is not difficult to do. We just need to provide surface areas for their growth.) Of course, we could just put chlorine or bleach in our tank, and that would take care of our bacterial problems. The unfortunate part of that is that it would also kill our fishes. There is a practical approach, however, and that is the ultra-violet light sterilizer.

An ultra-violet light sterilizer is effective because it kills everything, even viruses, but that means that you don't want it in your tank, because it would be harmful to the fishes. A good place to put the light is in the return line from your canister filter. You won't be able to use it if you only have an undergravel filter or if your carbon filter is the hang-on type. An ultra-violet light suitable for the marine aquarium is shielded to protect the animals it is not intended to harm—including us! That is, such a device can be harmful to our eyes. If it is placed in the return flow, the water being returned to the aquarium is not only clear and clean of harmful gases and organic compounds (thanks to the good quality activated carbon), it is also free of bacteria and viruses (thanks to the ultra-violet sterilizer).

Another piece of equipment to consider is an ozonizer. This is a generator that produces ozone gas. The gas is released right into the aquarium, and it kills bacteria, and it also oxidizes organic compounds and helps the redox potential of the tank. If you are a true technophile, you will have both an ultra-violet sterilizer and an ozonizer; however, if you want to choose between the two, my own preference is for the ultra-violet sterilizer. If the ozone isn't regulated just right, you could conceivably get a surplus of it in your living room or office. My personal preference is to keep the ozone up in the ozone layer, but, to be fair, many hobbyists are avid "ozonizers" and would be horrified by my opinion.

A piece of equipment that will work well with your ultra-violet sterilizer (or ozonizer) is a protein skimmer. These are also known as foam fractionators. The protein skimmer takes advantage of certain characteristics of large organic molecules, and their tendency to coat the surface of bubbles, to remove them from the aquarium. The protein skimmer can be designed for inside the aquarium use, but it looks better outside, and it is easier to clean and empty the foam cup there, too, so I recommend an outside model. A protein skimmer is a truly valuable piece of equipment, as it gets organic compounds out of your tank immediately and lessens the load on your filters. Like other pieces of equipment, it is most valuable when serviced regularly. The foam cup must be emptied almost daily, and the air bubbles must be checked to be sure that you are producing the proper amount for optimum fractionating.

Let's see now. We started out with a fish-only aquarium which was the essence of simplicity. It was to be filtered with an undergravel filter only. By now, we have added on a power filter with activated carbon. If we decide we want to utilize an

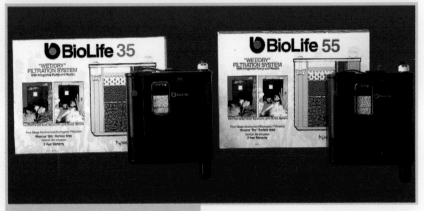

There are many wet/ dry filter systems available for purchase now. They come in different sizes so that they can be properly matched to your system. Photo courtesy Hagen.

Ozone generators are widely available and can be effective as destroyers of bacteria if common-sense precautions are taken during their use. Photo courtesy of Ultralife Reef Products.

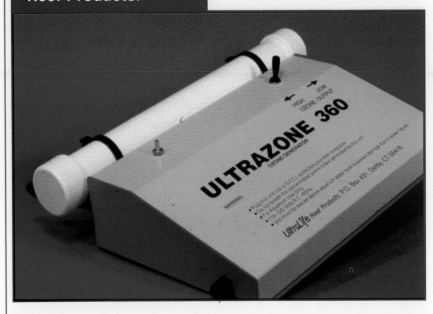

ultra-violet light sterilizer, we need to have our chemical filter contained in a canister with a pump, so that we can place the U-V sterilizer in the return hose of the canister. (You could have an ozonizer with simply an undergravel filter or with

an undergravel filter and outside filter combination.) We then added on a protein skimmer. The protein skimmer should either be in the intake line to the canister filter or it should take water directly from the tank and return it. We want the skimmer to process the water before it goes through any filtration.

If we are going to have an outside canister filter (or even if we are not), there is another consideration. We can set our undergravel filter up so that it is a reverse-flow system. That means that the water is pumped into the undergravel filter so that the water comes up through the gravel, rather than the other way around. Why do it that way? Because it keeps the gravel free of debris. At its simplest, the reverse-flow undergravel filter can consist of a powerhead with a sponge filter at the intake. The intake should always be low in the tank, regardless what system you utilize, as that is

Canister power filters are among the most popular of the outside filters. They are often used in tandem with other canister filters or with other filtering systems. Photo courtesy Hagen.

where the debris is most concentrated. With the powerheads and foam filters, it is possible to have reverse flow undergravel filtration as your only filter. Naturally, the foam filters must be changed frequently. This is a simple and workable system, but, remember, the more

devices you have to maintain water quality, the longer you will be able to keep your water in good quality and not have to change so much water so often.

A more complicated and more efficient reverse-flow undergravel system of filtration involves the use of at least two outside canister filters. The outflow tube of the canister filter goes right down the "lift tubes" to direct the water under the filter plate. The intake bar should be placed low in the tank, as was mentioned earlier, so that it picks up the debris where it is most concentrated. With a reverse-flow undergravel system, the subsand filter is pretty much relieved of its duty as a mechanical filter, and it is operating strictly as a biological filter for helping to maintain water quality. The gravel will rarely need cleaning as com-

pared to the normal undergravel filter.

Although this system may not seem simple with all the external canister filters, protein skimmers, and ultra-violet light sterilization, it is still relatively simple as compared with trickle filtration. And it is marvelously efficient, keeping the water sparkling clean, and, with proper use, the water quality will be maintained, too. In fact, with this system it is quite possible to have exceptionally large tanks.

TRICKLE FILTRATION

Although this is a particularly advantageous system for a living reef tank, I consider it an overcomplication for a fish-only tank. Naturally, there are those who disagree with me—some of them freshwater fish enthusiasts—but, in any case, the water won't be kept so clear unless you utilize a rapid-flow canister filter in conjunction with the system. In other words, to get all the advantageous of this system, you would need to add the trickle filtration system on to the one I have described. That is not the way it is generally done presently. In fact, most tanks with trickle filtation don't even have gravel. However, there is no reason you can't have both systems!

Decorative marine aquaria are available for reception rooms, offices, and the like, and many enhance the decor of a room in a private home. Courtesy Mr. & Mrs. Werther Paccagnella.

SETTING UP A FISH-ONLY TANK

size of the tank, it is generally recommended that you get as large a tank as you can afford or that you have the room for. The reasons for such recommendations are many. A large tank can

After you have made the choice to have your tank be one in which you will deliberately keep only fishes, the next decision is the size of your tank. (I say "deliberately" because it will unintentionally contain much life besides fishes, most of it microscopic.) Regarding the

Marine aquaria have to be set up according to the needs of the fishes that are being kept. Emblemaria piratula *is a small blenny that lives on a bottom that affords it numerous hiding places. Photo by Courtney Platt.*

give you a buffer, as changes take place more slowly in such a tank. But that is not completely true. If you keep big fish in a large tank, you can still get rapid changes in the quality of your water. The best reason for having a large tank is in order to keep larger fishes and give them the room they need. Too many people purchase tanks that are not large enough for *Holacanthus* angels, for example, with the idea that they will get a larger tank when the time comes. But it is easy to let the days slip by into months and not notice just how large the angels and tangs have grown.

The fact is you can have a small tank if you are willing to keep only small fishes in it and limit their number. And there are certain advantages to a small tank. You will be mixing up less water for the water changes, for example, and you can use smaller protein skimmers and other equipment that you have decided upon. A large filter will need changing less often, too, so a small tank is not something to avoid like the plague if it is appropriately stocked.

Nevertheless, a large tank in a proper setting can be breathtaking. A selection of fishes can be made that provides movement and color and that are not only esthetically pleasing, but they have

interesting behavior and biology. It is inevitable that you will learn something about the natural history of the fishes, for your guests will have lots of questions, and you won't want to disappoint them.

The major components of your decision of size of tank should be your financial capabilities, your interest in fishes (a lot of the interesting ones are not tiny), and the capacity of the room you plan to place it in. Whatever the size of the tank, the procedures will be pretty much the same.

YOUR SALT MIX

The synthetic sea salts available to marine hobbyists today are miles ahead of the salt mixes available when the hobby first started to get popular. Today's mixes are far superior in their capacity to sustain saltwater animals, whether they're fishes or invertebrates. They can be used to set up fish-only tanks, invertebrate-only tanks, or mini-reef tanks. They are good to the point that I'm not even going to mention the alternative of using natural sea water;

forget that.

Quite a few different mixes are on the market, and I think that I can safely say that if you're picking up at a pet shop or tropical fish specialty store one of the brands that's nationally advertised in aquarium magazines such as *Tropical Fish Hobbyist* you're going to be getting good stuff. The

Opsanus tau *is very tolerant of polluted conditions. It spawns in any available shelter, including conch shells and old cans. But it grows large (38 cm) and has a large mouth. Photo by Aaron Norman.*

brands vary in price and in their ease of mixing and of course in the claims that they make about what you can keep (and even breed) in them, so you have to make up your own mind about which one to use. Since probably not every brand is going to be avail-

Most marine aquaria utilize the artificial salt mixes on the market today. They allow the aquarist much more control over the physical parameters of the water than would be possible with natural water. Photo by Guy van den Bossche.

Artificial salts are widely available in a number of different formulations. Photo courtesy Coralife/ Energy Savers.

able to you anyway—dealers generally have a pretty wide selection, but it's unreasonable to expect them to carry every single brand on the market—you should ask your dealer for specific recommendations about which to use.

Your dealer's advice should be especially pertinent if his own marine setups are obviously thriving.

Keep in mind that price plays a part in synthetic sea salts as in most other products. Prices vary from manufacturer to manufacturer, naturally, and even individual manufacturers put out different salt mix products that vary in price according to their degree of refinement or how well buffered they are or what they include (such as additional trace elements and water conditioners) for added value. Again, to get a line on the comparative advantages of each such product and whether the extra cost is a worthwhile expenditure for you, check with your dealer.

Incidentally, no matter

which synthetic salt you select, do this:

FOLLOW THE MANUFACTURER'S DIRECTIONS for mixing and using. Don't take any shortcuts or cut out any needless steps or devise your own time-saving, labor-saving procedures. Follow the directions; they're there for good reason.

SETTING UP THE TANK

Unless you can be certain of getting acclimated fishes, a quarantine tank is a must. As a point of fact, a quarantine tank is one of the secrets to success with saltwater fishes. It must be remembered that most of your fishes are going to come from the wild and they have undergone the stresses of capture and shipment. Hence, they will be vulnerable to diseases, and the pathogens are likely to be inside their bodies and in the water in which they were caught. So get at least a small tank to be used just for acclimating any newcomers. It can be a mere 20-gallon tank; you can save the bulk of your

Fish-only tanks can include a wide selection of fishes. There is no need to worry about which fish might eat what invertebrates, a constant concern in a reef tank. Photo by Dr. Herbert R. Axelrod.

money for the main tank—whatever its size.

After deciding what size tank you want, the next decision is whether you want glass or acrylic. And this is not an easy decision either, as there are many adherents for both types. Generally speaking, though, acrylic tanks have been rapidly gaining in popularity. They are a little more expensive than glass tanks, but they are lighter and easier to handle. They are generally easier to work with in terms of drilling holes through the material, but you won't have to worry about that for the process I am going to describe now. Let us continue with our theme of keeping things simple, and I will assume that the tank will be a tank with an undergravel filter. I will go through setting up such a tank and then will discuss additional equipment in detail.

Even for a tank with undergravel filtration only, you will want to have equipment for monitoring your water. You should have a hydrometer for monitoring the salinity of your water. The hydrometer actually measures the specific gravity, but, by doing so, it indirectly gives you information about the amount of dissolved compounds in the water. You should also have test kits for measuring pH, nitrites, and nitrates. You will need non-toxic plastic buckets for mixing your ocean

water. Although small buckets will suffice, many hobbyists like to utilize large plastic trash bins which hold about five gallons. That can be handy, especially if you plan on keeping available replacement water on hand at all times—and that is not a bad idea. If your tap water is extremely hard or has undesirable compounds in it, you may want to use distilled water for your salt mix. This is rarely necessary, but, if it is, you may want to consider a reverse osmosis unit for

producing the water for your mix. The unit will also supply the proper water for replacement due to evaporation. In truth, really fussy hobbyists who want to keep

This double bubble aquarium was manufactured and designed by AAMPRO, Las Vegas, NV. It is about 125 x 60 x 250 cm (48 x 22 x 96 in) and comes complete with all the necessary filters, aerators, etc.

The aquarist must be constantly aware that the fishes that are kept in the confines of a home aquaria were once members of the reef community with a whole ocean at their disposal. Photo by M. P. & C. Piednoir.

air stones should be placed near the bottom of the lift tubes to get the maximum effect and the maximum water turnover.

We have already talked about the depth of the gravel bed. The question now is the composition of the gravel. Many marine aquarists simply won't have a substrate of anything other than coral sand. One reason for that predilection is that coral sand is considered more natural, and another is that the marine hobbyist is always concerned about maintaining pH in the saltwater aquarium, and coral sand helps a little in this, but good aquarium practices are the most important thing here. A good recommendation is a mixture of coral sand and oyster shell, but the most important thing is the size of the particles, in order to obtain the best flow of water through the particles without clogging. A particle size of $1/16$ to $3/16$ of an inch is the usual recommendation. Naturally, any type of gravel should be rinsed clean, but if you have oyster shell gravel as a component, you will never get an entirely clear runoff, as tiny particles of the material are always breaking off and producing the "milky" appearance; however, this won't be a problem in the aquarium, as the gravel won't be under the constant agitation that it is as you are washing it.

Whatever type of gravel you decide to use, it should be washed and placed over the filter plate and smoothed out to the two- to three-inch "ideal" depth that we are trying to maintain. (Just as a personal perspective here, I tend to err on the three-inch side, and I don't use a ruler, but you may want to for a while.) Now, you have

work. Leave the water about three inches from the top, as you want to leave room for your rocks and decorations.

Decorations are a matter of esthetics, but most marine aquarists want their tank to look as natural as possible. If the hobbyist is not a sport diver who has made at least one trip to a tropical sea, he or she may not be aware of what looks

dyed to look as though it is still alive.

Although it is a little more expensive, I personally prefer artificial ceramic coral. Such coral is much more life-like, and it adds a lot of color to the tank. Admittedly, so does dyed coral, and it is quite natural for coral to be broken off by tropical storms and washed up on shore. Conceivably, all coral for aquaria can come from such sources. Still, South Sea Islanders and, most especially, the people in the Philippines are desperately overcrowded, and the labor is there for harvesting the coral from nearly all the reefs. This would not happen for just marine aquaria, of course, but the aquarium hobby would get the blame. The truth is coral and shells are on sale in nearly every town all across the country, and nearly all of it comes from the burgeoning Philippines. As a "P. R." thing, if nothing else, I am strongly in favor of utilizing the ceramic coral. But I am only recommending, and I am not going to be indignant or self-righteous if I see coral skeletons in your tank.

Seahorses are safe for reef tanks and fish-only tanks. If kept in the latter they should be kept alone or housed only with similar delicate feeders. Photo by J. Kelly Giwojna.

your water mixed to a specific gravity of 1.020, and you pour that in the tank. Since you have carefully arranged your gravel, you will want to place a plate on the gravel to keep from undoing all your good

natural. The fact is that it is impossible to make it look completely natural, but we can heighten the impression. Certainly, the dead and bleached out coral that is seen in many tropical marine tanks is not natural looking. Many hobbyists nevertheless utilize these as decorations, and some at least allow copious algae to grow on the coral. This at least makes it look something like a coral rubble area or a dead reef area in the wild. A better approach is to buy coral that has been

In addition to coral, real or artificial, you can utilize rockwork in your tank, both for decoration and to provide shelter for your fishes. Many species do like hiding places, and the more they have, the better they are about leaving them to display for their tank mates and the aquarist.

When keeping seahorses it is necessary to provide something that they can anchor themselves on with their tails. Even so they may still cling to one another. Photo by Andre Roth.

CYCLING YOUR UNDERGRAVEL FILTER

In order to avoid "new tank syndrome" and having all your fishes die, you are going to need to get a culture of beneficial bacteria going to break down the waste products of your fishes. This is referred to as "cycling." A good plan is to get a tiny bit of gravel from an established undergravel marine filter and place it in your tank. Think of the bacteria as if they were fishes, and transport the gravel in a timely method, keeping it in good-quality marine water, as what you are really after are the beneficial bacteria, and they can die off just as easily as fishes under poor conditions (e.g. no water or poor quality water).

Now, what is usually referred to as a "quick pop" can be started by using ammonia. When the aquarium world first discovered, a couple of decades ago, just how a biological filter worked, hobbyists began keeping track of nitrates and nitrites and other metabolites, and when the filter began working at peak efficiency, this somehow became known as the filter having "popped."

When you get a "quick pop," what you are actually doing is cultivating the right bacteria for converting fish metabolites into less toxic compounds. You can more quickly get your filter into full working order by feeding it what it needs to prosper, and you don't have to risk any fish in the process. Simply add a few drops of ammonium chloride every other day for about twenty days (counting the in-between days). Test the nitrite level in the tank every three days—or even every day if you really want to keep tabs on it. It should build up and peak at about twenty days to a month and then decline. It will probably peak at about 18 ppm around the twentieth day, but many conditions affect that. Naturally, you want to keep everything just the way you will have it for the fishes, including the temperature of the water. In a few days after peaking the

A school of marine catfishes, Plotosus lineatus, is a very interesting sight, but it must be remembered that they have poisonous spines and must be handled with care. Photo by Mark Smith.

nitrite should be down to about 3 ppm or less.

At last we are ready for fishes.

A close-up of the head of a frogfish, Antennarius pictus. Frogfishes go "angling" for prey fishes with a "pole" and a "lure" which in reality are modified dorsal fin spines. Photo by M. P. & C. Piednoir.

COMPOUND FILTERS AND MAINTENANCE

tended merely as a discussion of extra gadgets for the marine aquarium and the advantages of each one. Even if you plan on keeping things simple and staying strictly with the undergravel filter, it is a good idea to know what

Now, the idea is to have marine fish keeping at its simplest. I am going to complicate things a tiny bit by discussing improvements to the traditional marine aquarium. These are not recommendations. What follows here is in-

If young fishes are maintained properly they will grow into fine adults. This French Angelfish (Pomacanthus paru) is in the transition stage from juvenile to adult color. Photo by Mike Mesgleski.

some of the equipment is and how it functions.

THE REVERSE-FLOW UNDERGRAVEL FILTER

The first apparatus under discussion here is not new equipment, but, rather, it is a variation on the tried-and-true undergravel filter. The reverse-flow undergravel filter is simply a filter in which the water is passed up through the gravel instead of down through it. Always implicit with this method of filtration was the presumption that the water would be filtered before being sent through the reverse-flow undergravel filter. The idea is to take some of the load off your most important biological filter. The undergravel filter functions as a mechanical filter and a biological filter. There could be some problem if the gravel gets clogged with debris and "dead spots" occur. With the reverse-flow filter, the idea is to mechanically filter the water before passing it through the gravel. This can be done by installing power heads that incorporate an intake tube covered with a sponge filter. This is simple mechanical filtration. It is important to have the intake down low in the tank, for that is where most of the debris can be picked up, as the fishes tend to stir it up just above the surface of the gravel.

Now, in order to have chemical filtration as well as mechanical filtration, you can utilize a canister filter for each lift tube. Naturally, you won't need as many lift tubes now, since you will be utilizing a more efficient means of moving the water than air stones. However, it is a good idea to have some aeration in addition to the water flow that is provided by the canister filters.

Many canister filters provide for biological filtration by supplying layers of "noodles" (little ceramic noodle-like units), "grass" (non-toxic plastic strings, looking very much like the fake grass in Easter Bunny baskets), and multi-layered pads. All these devices are simply to provide a habitat for the desirable denitrifying bacteria. This is in addition to a unit filled with activated carbon. In this case, you can eschew worrying about providing biological filtration in your canister filters, as you have a gravel bed for your biological filter. There is the theory, of course, that you simply can't get too much biological filtration, so many marine hobbyists utilize the biological components of their canister

filters. My own inclination is to simply use the canister filters as containers for mechanical and chemical filtration. That is, the canister filters are filled with nylon pads and activated carbon. As a matter of fact, I am inclined to utilize the carbon make-up which is combined with an ion-exchange resin. I have utilized such a combination since 1960, off and on,

The magenta and gold Gramma loreto does well in both reef and fish-only tanks. However, it will squabble with members of its own species. Photo by Mike Mesgleski.

and I have always been impressed at how well the pH stays steady, and the fishes seem to thrive, too. Way back 35 years ago when everyone was having so much trouble with marine tanks, I was impressed at how some tanks were able to prosper for two years without water changes, simply by utilizing

One of the cardinalfishes that is not so secretive is the Pajama Cardinal, Sphaeramia nematoptera. *Photo by Ken Lucas, Steinhart*

a combination undergravel filter and outside filter filled with an activated carbon and ion-exchange resin. (I remain an ardent advocate of partial water changes, however.)

Now, having said that, I should mention that I have had excellent results, and so have many fellow "mariners," by simply utilizing a filter cartridge in the power filters. It is important to change them regularly, but then it is important to change the carbon regularly, too. The main point of the reverse flow filter is to keep the particulate

matter separate from the biological filter, and whatever element you use in the canister filter will do that.

When you set up your reverse-flow undergravel filter with the use of canister filters, you can leave the intake the way it normally is, as it is nearly always a grated intake positioned relatively low in the tank. However, you won't be utilizing the spray bar in the return. The return tube will go down the lift tubes. Since you won't be having bubbles coming out of those tubes, you can take the top off of them. Place the return tube all the way down to the filter plate, and fix it in place with a plastic tie-down up near the top of the lift tube. (Fortunately, with the growing popularity of reverse-flow undergravel

filters, manufacturers have designed their canister filters with an apparatus that fits right over the tops of the lift tubes so that you won't have to go to all the "fuss" just described. However, you may have to special order these special adapters.)

With the reverse-flow filter, the gravel will be more efficient as a biological filter, as the gravel will have much less tendency to accumulate debris. Also, your gravel will need cleaning much less frequently, since the water is "scrubbed" first before it is passed through the gravel. There will be some accumulation of detritus simply because of the excrement of the fishes and the inevitable leftover food, but if you simply siphon (or hydrovacuum) the bottom of the tank on a regular basis, even that will be extremely minimal.

Are there disadvantages to the reverse-flow undergravel filter? For every action there is a reaction, as Sir Isaac Newton said, and it is true that there are some disadvantages to the reverse-flow undergravel filter. For one thing, you have complicated things, either by the power heads or the outside canister filters. Everything else being equal, we want to keep things as simple as possible, but the advantages of the reverse-flow filter are certainly sufficient to at least give a marine hobbyist pause to consider it. A further disadvantage is that we are missing out on the benefit of the undergravel filter as a mechanical filter. There aren't many filters that can clear up a cloudy aquarium as well as an undergravel filter, for all the water is rapidly being passed down through the gravel. That, in effect, accelerates the natural settling propensity of debris. This will no longer be the case with the reverse-flow version, but if the elements of the canister filter or the sponges on the power lift are changed regularly, you won't have to complain about debris in your tank, as the water will appear so clear that the fish will seem to be suspended in air.

PROTEIN SKIMMER

The protein skimmer is sometimes called a water fractionator, and it works on the principle that it is easy to create bubbles in ocean water, and there is a collection of organic material at the surface of those bubbles. If the bubbles are collected in a cup or have an overflow to dispose of them, organic molecules can be removed before they even become part of the nitrogen cycle. In other words, one of the main advantages of the protein skimmer is that it greatly reduces the load on your biological filter. So efficient are many protein skimmers that they have become quite popular with all marine aquarists, from fish enthusiasts to invertebrate devotees to living reef connoisseurs.

One reason that the protein skimmer is mentioned first of the auxiliary equipment available is that it can be so effective and can really help you keep the redox potential of your tank up there where you want it. It would be the first bit of auxiliary equipment that I would consider to "complicate" our simple system

(after the reverse-flow undergravel filter). The advantages are that the protein skimmer pulls the organics right out of the water before they have a chance to break down into harmful components. That takes a load off your undergravel filter and off your mechanical and chemical filters, too. The disadvantage is that it is a further complication, and it is a device that needs daily

Apogon pseudomaculatus is one of the typical red colored cardinalfishes that will hide during the day but will come out to feed at night. Feeding schedules should be adjusted accordingly. Photo by K. Knaack.

attention. The air bubbles have to be just right, and the cup should be emptied daily. The device should be monitored daily, too, to be sure that the foam is going into the cup or overflow device at the right consistency. You don't want to be losing your water, and you

Pygoplites diacanthus add a lot of color to a marine tank (as do most angelfishes). This is one of those angelfishes that do not change color drastically with age. Photo by M. P. & C. Piednoir.

don't want the bubbles sliding right back into the tank again.

It will take time working with your device for you to get to the point that you are truly proficient at having the protein skimmer work at its best. It is difficult to designate a specific bubble size, but a profusion of small bubbles is generally preferred. However, if the bubbles are too small, the foam may not form properly or the bubbles may be less persistent. If the bubbles are too large, they rise too quickly through the tube and the discharge is too watery. A little experimentation will help you decide what size bubble and rate of flow is best for your system.

Some excellent protein skimmers are available. I prefer the venturi pump-driven protein skimmers which are always situated outside the tank. There are also some excellent counter-current skimmers that are designed for outside the tank. The water goes to the protein skimmer and back to the tank via the power of the pump in the protein skimmer. Protein skimmers designed for use inside the tank are generally less expensive, but they are difficult to service (which you have to do daily), and the water level in the tank has to be kept at a crucial level for the device (although some inside skimmers are on brackets so that you can adjust the skimmer to the water level, but that is a pain, too).

Besides the fact that an inside protein skimmer takes away from the natural look of the aquarium, its height is limited by that of the tank. That affects its efficiency, as the higher the tube the longer the bubbles are in contact with the water and the more efficient your protein skimming. Although an outside skimmer is more expensive, it has a lot to ber are the ones recommended, and I particularly like the ones with an activated carbon filter in the return lines, as that helps contain the ozone in the reaction chamber.

As is the case with the ultraviolet sterilizer, the ozone sterilizer complicates your system, but it has its beneficial aspects (as is the case with the U-V sterilizer), for not only does it help keep down the bacterial and parasitic populations, it helps increase the redox potential of the tank by breaking down the molecules of organic compounds.

FLUIDIZED BED BIOLOGICAL FILTERS

While I said that I would be discussing different pieces of equipment in order of what I considered the most important (with the least important being last), this is an outstanding exception to that statement. Why not list this first then? Well, it is a relatively new system, but everything that I have experienced and all my discussions with people and all my readings indicate that this new system is a spectacular biological filter. It consists of a bed of relatively small gravel that is kept in a state of constant movement, with a good portion of it being suspended in the water. There is a built-in pump that directs a spray or sprays of water at a strategic point or points, and the filter me-

dium (usually fine beach sand) is contained in a holder shaped like and upside-down pyramid. If nothing else, this filter is fun to watch. While not actually new, it has taken some time for this type of filter to be properly sized and adapted to the home aquarium.

One of the main points of this device is that all the filter medium is utilized and is active in the process of biological filtration. (It is worth noting here that, of course, the gravel merely provides a "home" for the beneficial bacteria. What this filter does is provide the bacteria equal exposure to any nutrients available.) An important point here is that "dead spots" are virtually non-existent. That was one of the goals when I recommended the reverse-flow undergravel filter. My perspective in recommending systems has been simplicity, effectiveness, and initial outlay of expense. That is why I described the regular undergravel filter first. It is simple, inexpensive, and it is effective; however, it is notorious for developing dead spots. Of course, the reader was informed as to how to deal with these in the case of the "normal"

undergravel filter. The point here is that the fluidized bed biological filter seems to need virtually no maintenance. There is the usual maintenance situation of occasionally having to replace the built-in pump in due course, but such things are to be expected.

Filefishes, like this **Cantherhines macrocerus,** *are a bit less aggressive than their cousins the triggerfishes, but they are nippy and must be watched closely when kept with less aggressive fishes. Photo by Courtney Platt.*

These filters are currently being manufactured to draw water from the sump of the wet/dry filter or from the return tube of a canister filter. An important point here is that the water should be filtered before being introduced to the fluidized filter. This filter functions only as a biological filter, not a mechanical one. But its biological filtering powers are astounding. My personal preference is to use it as a companion to the reverse-flow undergravel filter, but it could only be used in conjunction with the return tubes from the canister filters. At least there is no way I can envision utilizing a power head that was designed for the reverse-flow filter. This may change as demand for this new filter increases, but I am not sure that a mere foam prefilter would be sufficient filtration for these devices. Any debris whatsoever could cause clogging.

One of the most significant problems with any conventional biological filter is that the layers of bacteria that accumulate on the surface of the media can get quite thick, thereby blocking the transfer of nutrients and oxygen to the lower layers. In time, this results in a colony of mature bacteria that consume fewer nutrients than a young culture. Because of the constant movement of the medium, there is a constant sloughing of older layers of bacteria which ensures that those present are younger and more efficient "converters."

Fluidized bed biological filters have more surface area than any other type of biological filter. Because of this, they can be compactly designed. There is virtually no maintenance involved. In short, these fluidized filters can handle just about anything. They do more work, cost less, and require less maintenance than all other biological filters. The only reason I didn't feature them here is that I am naturally cautious. There have been so many wonder devices that didn't quite live up to what we had hoped for. But, based on current knowledge and the experience of fish shops and

The Red Hind (Epinephelus guttatus) is very colorful and does well in captivity. But it does grow to 18 inches so a very large tank is needed. Photo by Courtney Platt.

problem is to have a very deep medium so that the bacteria can thrive at the bottom. Still, the wet portion of the filter generally seems to function better separately, and some manufacturers produce such a filter that can either be placed beneath the gravel in the tank or have its own (very slow!) water supply.

COMPOUND FILTERS

Although, as we have seen, the various filters and devices often have their own idiosyncratic requirements as to water flow, the convenience of having everything incorporated into one flow system has inspired manufacturers to produce wet/dry filters that have everything contained within them—even the heater. Such devices have a cup-like take up system from the aquarium which skims water from the surface (where the most metabolic compounds are likely to be), and runs the water through some mechanical filter, such as nylon wool, then goes to a drip plate or rotating spray bar, then through bioballs, coiled matting, or other inert material, then through a chemical filter, and then into the sump in which there may be a protein skimmer as well as a wet filter medium.

There are disadvantages to such a com-

pound filter, of course. The main problem is that nearly every unit is compromised somewhat because of the requirements of the other. For example, it would be best to have the mechanical and chemical filter be placed before the inlet to the trickle filter, but the flow would be too fast for that class of filter. As it is, of course, the flow is too fast for the maximum performance of the wet portion of the filter. And a protein skimmer needs a "crack" at the water before any filtration at all! Nevertheless, the convenience of this set up outweighs the problems in the opinion of many hobbyists.

DISADVANTAGES TO SYSTEMS

Nothing is perfect in this world, so I have listed some of the disadvantages of the various systems and devices I have described just so we don't get too excited about any one system and become blinded to its faults. While these comments are not intended to impeach any system (the undergravel filter, for example, of which I am a great advo-

cate), it is felt that they will help hobbyists or potential hobbyists make decisions about equipping their aquarium, or aquaria, as the case may be.

Undergravel Filter

Undergravel filters are notorious for becoming clogged with debris. They, thus, become virtual sewers within the aquarium, and they tend to channel the flow of

A male Princess Parrotfish (Scarus taeniopterus). Like wrasses, parrotfishes have a "super male" with bright colors that will spawn one-on-one with a female, rather than in a group. Photo by Courtney Platt.

water. The surface area in an undergravel filter can be quite substantial, depending on the size of gravel used and the depth of the gravel bed. Upwards of 450-650 square feet per cubic foot is possible. However, unless the filter is cleaned regularly, not all of

Nocturnal fishes are generally some shade of red and have large eyes. This Bigeye (Priacanthus cruentatus) is quite typical. Don't expect to see much of it during the daytime. Photo by Courtney Platt.

the surface will be utilized because of the channeling of the water from the clogging. Uneven flow patterns are possible even with a reverse-flow system, although they are minimized considerably. The initial outlay for these filters is the least expensive compared with any other filtration system, so that is definitely <u>not</u> a fault.

Protein Skimmers

These require daily inspection and maintenance. The bubbles must be checked and adjusted and the foam cup must be emptied. Although one of the good things about the protein skimmer, besides the fact that it gets rid of metabolic compounds before they can become a problem, is that they provide good aeration. That is also the bad news, as all that bubbling tends to increase the evaporation, so the water level of the tank must be watched assiduously, and the salinity should be checked often.

Chemical Filters

Although these devices remove harmful gases and metabolic compounds, they also remove some of the beneficial trace elements. A routine replenishing of the trace elements will help alleviate this fault. Another problem is that, if the filter material is not changed regularly and frequently, the filter medium can slough off a lot of the material it has collected and thus become a problem instead of a help.

Canister Filters

These need regular cleaning, and they are not easy to disconnect without making a mess. (It **is** possible however!) One of their problems is that they are out of sight, so it is easy to forget about them.

GENERAL TANK MAINTENANCE

There is something magical about aeration. Tanks seem to do better with lots of it. One of the reasons, of course, is that aeration helps get dissolved oxygen into the water. And even if you don't have a protein skimmer aeration helps

Lets assume, at first, that you have the simplest set up, a tank with the "regular" undergravel filter and no peripherals or compound filters. A good combination here is to have the outside lift tubes powered by power heads and the two (or more) inside ones with air stones.

Scarus vetula *nibbling away at some coral. Through this action parrotfishes are responsible for reducing much of the coral to sand. Photo by Courtney Platt.*

Such conditions are rare, and good aquarium practices will usually exclude the problem.

If you are using a reverse-flow filter with either power heads or outside canister filters, you, once again, will be doing yourself and your fishes a favor by supplying aeration via an auxiliary air pump. In this case, you most definitely don't want to place air stones in the supplementary lift tubes, as you would then be working against your main filter. It

will be to your advantage to have the air stones positioned toward the center of the tank away from the edges of the tank so that salt deposits won't form at the top of your aquarium along the edges and start salt creep down the sides. The trouble is the air stones are difficult to position toward the center, and they don't look natural there anyway. One way around this problem is to place them at the base of a real or artificial coral. Place them out of sight at the back of the coral ornament, and the fine bubbles coming up won't look that out of place, as such bubbles actually occur in nature, although it is not usually on a continuous basis. Anyway, it is not a displeasing sight, and it

will be beneficial for your fishes.

If you decided to go with a protein skimmer, check it daily to make sure that the bubbles are of the right size and that the flow is right. Experience will help you learn the combination of these two parameters that helps produce the most foam. Empty your foam

"Check your protein skimmer daily to be sure it is functionng properly."

collection cup daily. Don't worry if there is not lots of productive foam even after you have experimented around and found the best combination of flow and bubbles. If your aquarium practices are so good that your water is constantly of excellent quality, the chances are that you don't have enough organic matter in your water to produce the vile foam you are trying to get—and that is good! Chances are, though, that there will be times when you are getting all-too-productive foam! This is only natural.

Amphiprion ocellaris is one of those marine fishes that are being raised commercially. These farmed fish usually command a higher price than wild caught individuals. Feeding them is not difficult. Photo by Andre Roth.

This will especially be the case if you are trying to give your fishes the ultimate in a nutritious diet.

FEEDING

Ideally, marine fishes should be fed four times a day, for they do browse pretty much continuously on the reef. This is not possible for everyone, and that is understandable. We may be dedicated to our bit of the ocean in the living room or office, but we have to work to help support it, too! One excellent compensation for not feeding that often is to place a leaf of romaine lettuce in the tank daily. It does not need to be either frozen or scalded as is so often recommended. It merely needs to be weighed down or attached to one of your ornaments. Nearly all the fish will go crazy over it, and the romaine will definitely show the effects of the nibbling by evening, and it should be removed at that time.

The fish should be fed a combination of dry and frozen foods, with occasional treats of live food. Fortunately, there are excellent formulated foods on the market, both frozen and dry, that have the essential amino acids and vitamins for marine fish species. If your fishes will eat pellets, and most of them will, these tend to be especially beneficial for marine fishes and keeps

Shelves in well stocked pet shops are brimming with a wide variety of foods especially designed for marine fishes. Besides staple foods there are numerous specialty items available. Photo courtesy of Hagen.

them fleshed out nicely. Ideally, the tank should be vacuumed about fifteen minutes after each feeding, as many marine fishes are not good about scavenging off the bottom. This is merely an ideal and not a maxim or a necessary practice for the successful maintenance of marine fish species. The ideal is always mentioned here as a basis for orienting your own activities so that you know about how far you are straying from ideal practices. And, quite frankly, even ideal practices are a little subjective, as many hobbyists would be aghast at vacuuming the bottom only fifteen minutes after feeding, for many angels, damsels, and surgeons will graze upon detritus. Nonetheless, we all know that there is an extremely delicate balance between providing the fishes with a nutritious diet and polluting the tank (however minor) from overfeeding. And this is one case in which the protein skimmer is a real ace-in-the-hole, as a protein skimmer will pull out much of the organic waste from overfeeding before it has a chance to start to break down.

Algae in a fish-only tank is rarely a problem. In fact, it provides the animals something to nibble on. There is a symbiotic relationship of sorts between the coral reefs and many of the coral reef fishes, for algae would be deadly to the corals, as it would shield them from the all-important sunlight that they themselves need to live. Thus, surgeons and damsels, among others, help keep the algae from overcoming the corals. Of course, their job is made easier by the fact that the water is so sterile of the nutrients necessary for plant life.

In any case, it is a good idea to merely clean off the front glass of algae and allow it to grow on all the other surfaces, as the fishes will most likely keep it in check. And the algae, together with the especially-formulated foods for marine fishes, will keep them pretty and happy.

As for live foods, most marine hobbyists are skittery about utilizing adult brine shrimp because it is harvested from the wild and may be a conduit of pathogens or parasites. True enough, brine shrimp are found in waters too saline for fishes to live in; hence, the parasites and pathogens lack a host in those waters. However, the cysts for both bacteria and protozoans can be quite tolerant of such conditions, and they, thus, could be transported with the brine shrimp. One precaution is to keep the brine shrimp in fresh water for several hours, but even this does not satisfy all marine hobbyists.

The fact is that a surprisingly large number of marine fish species will eat the newly-hatched brine shrimp, and these are free of pathogenic organisms. And they may be just more nutritious, too, as *Artemia* have an especially nutrient-laden yolk sack that is present before the first molt of these animals. The marine hobbyist can merely hatch out a batch of brine shrimp a couple of times a week and provide the aquarium denizens with a treat that is both nutritious and a change of pace.

Whatever you feed, it is always a good idea to at least glance in the tank 15 minutes later to be sure that there is no uneaten food at the bottom of the tank. If you are using canister filters or other peripherals, such as an ozonizer, be aware of the intakes for these devices when you feed live food, and try to place it in an area in which it won't be immedi-

Good basic aquarium hygiene is essential. But the aquarist must also be concerned with a little cleaning for pure esthetic reasons, like removing the algae from the front glass. There are many tools available to help make this chore easier. Photo courtesy Aquarium Pharmaceuticals.

ately sucked out.

It is only common sense that good basic aquarium hygiene and good aquarium practices will help stave off the heavy duty cleaning sessions. And they will make life much easier for your fishes—and for you.

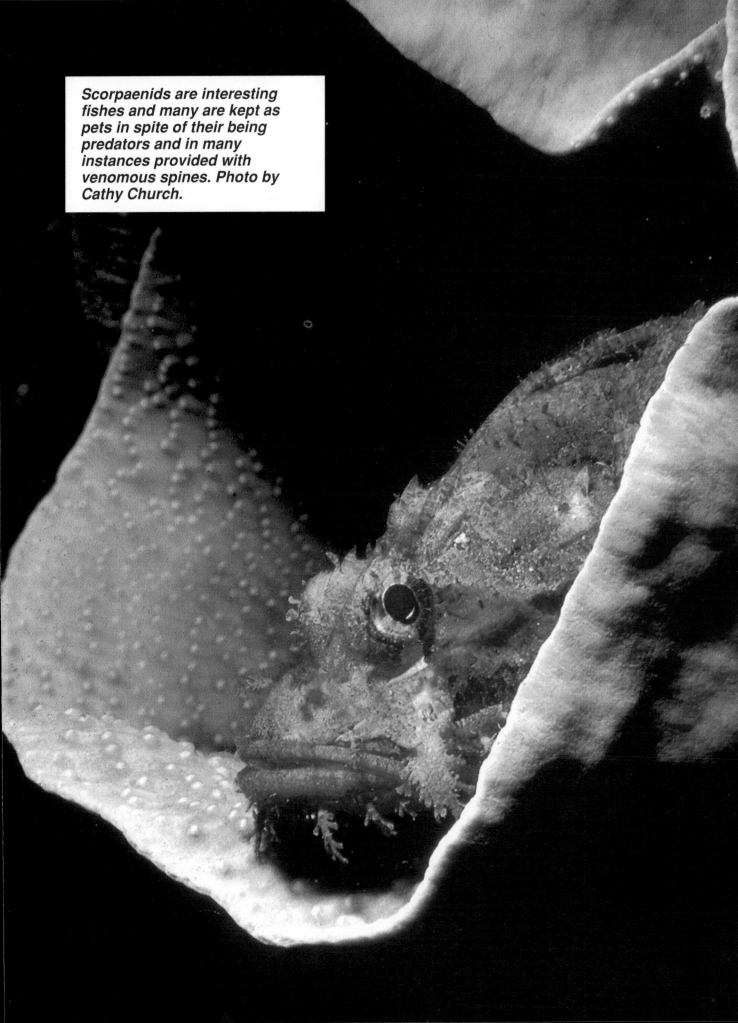

Scorpaenids are interesting fishes and many are kept as pets in spite of their being predators and in many instances provided with venomous spines. Photo by Cathy Church.

COMMUNITY TANK: SOME SUGGESTIONS

many fish enthusiasts simply start out wanting a beautiful moving picture in the living room. They probably saw someone else's community tank and were taken with the beauty and novelty of it. At least, it seems to me that

Tropical fish hobbyists go through several stages, and perhaps that is good, for it is that fact that probably keeps their interest in their hobby fresh and maintains in them a love of life in general which is the envy of many. In any case,

The selection of fishes for a marine aquarium is critical. An incompatible combination can be devastating. Learn as much as possible about the fishes that are to be kept — habits, food and feeding, etc. — and use this information to advantage. Photo of an Oxymonacanthus longirostris *by M. P. & C. Piednoir.*

Platax orbicularis.

Echidna nebulosa. *Photo by Aaron Norman.*

Zebrasoma xanthurum. *Photo by M. P. & C. Piednoir.*

Halichoeres hortulanus. *Photo by Roger Steene.*

Platax pinnatus. *Photo by Earl Kennedy.*

Gomphosus varius. *Photo by Dr. Shih-chieh Shen*

French)
Three blue tangs
One bird wrasse (or
   lyretailed, paddlefin, or
   banana wrasse)
One batfish

200-gallon Tank
Six blue damsels (or bue-
   green reeffish)
Three common
   clownfishes
One royal gramma

One koran angel (and
   one blue face,
   imperator, gray, or
   French)
Three blue tangs
One bird wrasse (and
   one lyretailed,
   paddlefin, or banana
   wrasse)
One batfish
One snowflake eel
One zebra moray

300-gallon Tank
Six blue damsels (or
   blue-green reeffish)
Three common

clownfishes
One royal gramma
One koran angel (and
   one of the following:
   blue face, imperator,
   gray, or French)
Three blue tangs
One bird wrasse (and
   one lyretailed,
   paddlefin, or banana
   wrasse)
One batfish
One snowflake eel
One zebra moray

500 Gallon Tank

Six blue damsels (or
   green chromis)
Three common
   clownfishes
One royal gramma
One koran angel (and
   two picks of the follow-
   ing: blue face,
   imperator, gray, or
   French)
Three blue tangs
One bird wrasse, one
   lyretailed wrasse, one
   paddlefin wrasse, and
   one banana wrasse
One batfish
One snowflake eel
One zebra moray

Notes on the Selection

This list was made out with
the help of seasoned amateur
and professional marine
aquarists. The idea is to have
a group of compatible fishes
that also are relatively hardy
and are good-looking, to boot.
And they look good together,
too, as the color scheme is
right—at least, in most
people's eyes! The angels and
wrasses are tricky to combine,
and they should most cer-
tainly be introduced in even
the biggest tanks at the same
time.

All the species included in
these lists are universally
considered to be hardy. That
is why the yellow tang is not
listed even though it is commonly seen in shops. That
doesn't mean that you
shouldn't give the species a
try once you have gained
some experience and confi-
dence. However, among
marine hobbyists, they are
often referred to as the "ca-

naries of the tank," as they
will be the first to die if your
water conditions are slipping.

No problem fishes are
included, and that means
even triggerfishes. Yes, I must
confess to being a little "trigger
happy" myself, but they are
not recommended for trouble-
free tanks. The thing about it
is that triggers are not really
as aggressive as many damsels, but they can do horrendous damage with their
powerful jaws, and it can all
happen
quickly.
If you
want to
include
a trigger
in your
commu-
nity
tank
after
this
caveat,
the best
bet is
the blue
trigger
or
*Odonus
niger* (so
named because it turns black
in preservative).

The zebra moray and
snowflake moray are specialized mollusk eaters, but they
have been known to take
fishes at night, so there
should be a minor caveat in
regard to them, too. Of
course, it won't seem like a
minor problem if you lose
some valuable fishes. What I
mean is that it is a potential
problem, something that may
never happen, but something

of which you should be
aware. It is not intended that
these lists be slavishly ad-
hered to; they are intended
merely as a guide. These are
combinations that have
worked many times for many
different people.

The following catalogue of
fishes includes many species
not suited for the community
aquarium. The species is
listed because of the fact that
it is generally available, and
the hobbyist may want to

*If you want to include a
triggerfish in your
community tank your
best bet is* Odonus
niger. *Photo by M. P. &
C. Piednoir.*

include it in some special
assortment—or keep it by
itself, for that matter.

A final comment is in
order. Beauty is certainly
subjective. But to most
people, there is nothing
more beautiful than the

combination of common clownfishes and blue damsels. On the other hand, angels are wildly popular because of their exotic shape and beautiful coloration. One of the most beautiful and practical species from the standpoint of size and hardiness is the royal gramma (*Gramma loreto*). Many may wonder why only one is recommended per tank. And there is the rub! This beautiful little fish is extremely aggressive toward others of its species in an aquarium. As a diver, you wonder how that can be. For in Caribbean waters you see them together in coral heads or reefs, each with its own cave to which it retreats frequently and can be seen inside almost invariably upside down. This knowledge only makes more frustrating the fact that they are so difficult to keep together in captivity.

Of course, there is a reason why this species behaves as it does. The congregations found in nature, often numbering up to a hundred, were formed naturally, and there is some aggression between them, but a hierarchy has already been established, and the fish all "know" each other. When the fishes are collected, they are rarely kept together. Hence, if you try to place them in your tank, you have placed "strangers" together, each bent on establishing dominance. For that reason, the species is pretty much banned in

groups in the community tank. That does not mean, however, that some aquarist with a particular penchant for royal grammas will not come along and find a way to keep these beautiful creatures together, and, perhaps, even to spawn them. Certainly, they are worth study and worth taking a chance on, as they would surely command a respectable price, being one of the most beautiful of all creatures.

Speaking of breeding marine fishes, there is a concerted trend among marine fish hobbyists to at least attempt this with some species. There are three reasons for this: First, it is now known that it can be done. It was once thought impossible, as marine fishes nearly all have a larval form that is dispersed to the planktonic rafts of the ocean. During this time the larvae are part of the plankton, and they may have specialized feeding needs which change as they develop. Some species spend more time in the planktonic larval stage than others, and the shorter the planktonic larval time, the better the chances of the hobbyist being able to spawn and raise the species involved. In any case, many species have been spawned, including clownfishes and angels.

The most success or the most effort has been devoted to the various species of

clownfishes, as these are nearly always available. They often cost a little more, but they are worth the extra price! It is strongly recommended that the hobbyist buy "tank raised" species whenever possible. They are more hardy, more colorful, and they are easier to keep in groups without horrendous fighting. Not only that, but they are descended from parents that spawned in captivity. That means that if you decide to give spawning them a try, it should be easier than if you just raised fishes that had been caught in the ocean.

Still, it must be emphasized that even clownfishes are quite a challenge to spawn. (Actually, it is not the spawning part that is so difficult, it is the raising of the fry!) But that simply makes the accomplishment all the sweeter, and it is a valuable contribution to the hobby.

Although there are those who contend that the marine component of the hobby did not become legitimate until the spawning of species in captivity took place, that view is a little provincial. Certainly, the captive breeding of species is extremely important and, most decidedly, desirable, but many hobbyists simply want a display of a bit of the fabulous ocean for their living room or office, and they can't be faulted for that. It is hoped that the suggested combinations will be of value for such aquarists.

Many marine fishes are imported as juveniles as they usually adapt better to captivity and have room to grow. This rare Zebrasoma gemmatum *juvenile* should grow to a length of about 22 cm. Photo by Aaron Norman.

FISHES FOR THE MARINE AQUARIUM

Finally, some species are included that have historically had a fascination for hobbyists, either because of their unique biology or because of their unusual or entertaining behavior. For convenience, the fishes are

The emphasis here is on fishes that will do well in community aquaria; however, some species are included because

The number and type of fishes that can be placed in a reef tank is limited since the aquarist has to worry about the fishes eating the invertebrates. There is much more freedom in selecting fishes for a fish-only tank. Photo by M. P. & C. Piednoir.

they appear regularly on retailer's lists. Also, some non-community species are included for just the general interest of the aquarist.

listed primarily by family, although sometimes the order and even the super-class, class, and/or sub-class, has to be mentioned. Remember, the family name always ends in "idae."

The assumption is strong that most hobbyists who are interested enough in the marine hobby to read a book on it are people who have already had experi-ence with freshwater tropi-cal fishes, and, thus, know something about fishes. Granting, however, that some hobbyists have the temerity to jump straight into the marine hobby and often have the audacity to succeed at it, I would first like to give a little general background information about fishes.

First of all, is there a difference between marine fishes and their freshwater counterparts? The fact is that there are some families of fishes that have both marine and freshwater representatives. Neverthe-less, there are distinct families of only marine and only freshwater fishes. But the history of the different freshwater families varies, so that some are referred to as primary freshwater fishes, while others are called secondary freshwater fishes (for example cichlids) because they originated from marine ancestors. Also, various marine forms have colonized freshwater areas. Some of them, such as puffers, have established permanent residency and

even have an endemic form in Lake Tanganyika. Bull sharks inhabit Lake Managua, and it took ichthyologists quite some time to determine that they migrate in and out of the lake and that the bull shark was not a separate freshwater species. Con-versely, freshwater fishes

These fishes have been attracted to their own images when a mirror was placed in their aquarium. Some of them were ready to do battle with the new "rival" that suddenly appeared. If this is tried be sure the mirror does not contain any toxin that will poison the tank. Photo by Joachim Frische.

have made inroads into the ocean. Some species, such as salmon, live their adult life in the ocean but mi-grate to fresh water to spawn, and the young spend much of their grow-

ing time there. But species that can move freely from marine to fresh water are limited in number.

What is the barrier then? Why can't all fish species migrate back and forth?

Part of the answer is in the nature of their body fluids. We all know that we humans can't drink ocean water—at least, not very much of it, and not on a regular basis. The problem is concerned with osmotic pressure. Ocean water is more dense than our blood, so drinking the water actually dehydrates us. Fishes are more of an integral part of the water than we are, and osmotic pressure is therefore even more important to them. Consequently, freshwater and marine fishes each have a problem. In the case of freshwater fishes the osmotic pressure is inward. Water passes through the membranes of the gills and other parts of the body. The

A Long-nosed Hawkfish (Oxycirrhites typus) caught by the camera flash in front of a large gorgonian. Photo by Cathy Church.

problem for freshwater fishes, then, is too much water, so they do not actively drink water, and they have extremely efficient kidneys in order to keep expelling the excess water without losing important body concentrates. With marine fishes, the problem is not enough water. The pressure is outward. Thus, marine fishes are constantly losing water and must constantly drink water to replace that which

is lost. They have specialized structures (usually on the roof of the mouth and on the gills) to excrete the excess salt. So, if someone tells you that you "drink like a fish," ask them "Saltwater or fresh?" before determining whether it is an insult!

Nearly all the fish species that marine hobbyists want to keep are coral reef fishes. That is because they are the most colorful and have the most exotic shapes. One reason that this is so is that the coral reefs have been around for so long that they have provided a long-term, stable environment to which the fishes could

evolve specialized adaptations. And that is the reason why so many species are more of a challenge to successfully keep, too, as it is difficult to reproduce the most stable environment on Earth — and keep it that way. The fact that marine tropical fish hobbyists routinely accomplish this feat is a tribute to the desirability of the fishes and the ingenuity of humankind.

SHARKS, SKATES, AND RAYS (CLASS CHONDRICHTHYES: SUBCLASS ELASMOBRANCHII)

Actually, this is a class (or subclass of fishes) of animals that are hardly considered suitable for home aquaria, and yet many are available to the hobbyist. The fact is that sharks have been successfully kept by the home aquarist. And, to tell the truth, these are among the most interesting of animals. They have been around for an extremely long time, dating back to before the time of the dinosaurs. This extended time period has allowed extremely interesting adaptations to have evolved. For example, all sharks have internal fertilization, but some still lay eggs. Others are not only livebearers, but some of them have a placental system of nourishing the embryo that is quite analogous to that of the mammals. Not only that, but many species of shark have a slow growth rate to sexual maturity, up to at least a decade. Add to that the fact that some sharks have only one or two pups, and we see that we have very successful animals here.

Another interesting feature of the sharks is the fact that they have a very large brain for their body size. In fact, it corresponds to such terrestrial animals as birds and mammals. A large brain doesn't necessarily mean high intelligence, however. The largeness of the brain could have evolved for processing the information that comes from the extra senses that the shark possesses. In any case, these are highly

evolved animals, beautifully adapted to their environment. The fact that they have an adjustable aperture to the eye (i.e. the pupil), in contradistinction to nearly all other species of fishes, is testament to their complexity.

The reason most hobbyists even think of keeping a shark in their tanks is that the word shark sends fear into the minds of the general public, as the "Jaws" movies and general sensationalistic reporting has everyone thinking that these animals threaten the extinction of *Homo sapiens*. In actual fact, it is the other way around. Very few species of sharks are even dangerous to humans, and certainly humans are not the natural food of any species of shark. The ones that could be dangerous to man are pretty much in the open ocean. They do not patrol the shores looking for waders! On the other hand, humans relentlessly hunt sharks with factory type fishing and drift nets. Perhaps more than any other group of fishes, sharks are threatened by humans, for shark species have a late-developing reproductive cycle

and do not mass produce young. It will truly be a shame if we drive sharks to extinction, for not only are they magnificent creatures that serve an important function in the marine ecosystem, but there is so

The most popular ray for marine aquaria is the colorful blue-spotted ray (Taeniura lymma). Photo by Dr. Herbert R. Axelrod at Marau.

much that we can learn from them. Their immune system, for example, seems to be more effective than ours.

The Chondrichthyes have employed a unique device to cope with the problem of water loss through osmosis (a problem for all marine fishes, since the blood is less dense than ocean water). Their blood contains large quantities of dissolved urea which, in combination with trimethylamine oxide and the ordinary blood salts, keeps the body in osmotic

With an adult wingspan of up to 250 cm and some dangerous barbs at the base of the tail the spotted eagle ray (Aetobatus narinari) is only suitable for large public aquaria. Photo by Courtney Platt.

balance with sea water. This means that these fishes don't have to develop specialized cells or organs for excreting salts, as do the marine bony fishes.

A strength and a weakness of the sharks, skates, and rays is the cartilaginous skeleton. It is a positive feature in that it imparts strength and flexibility, thus providing many of the animals with amazing agility and suppleness. On land, however, sharks must be

The horn sharks are not active swimmers, spending most of their time sitting on the bottom. This is Heterodontis zebra, one of the more popular species. Photo by K.-H. Choo.

handled carefully so as not to rupture any part of the skeleton of cartilage.

SHARKS

Nurse Sharks (Orectolobidae)

Most pelagic sharks cannot be kept in the home aquarium because they do not have efficient enough breathing mechanisms. They don't need them since they are constantly on the move in the open ocean, taking in sufficient oxygen bearing water as they move. However, inshore species, such as the nurse shark, have developed more efficient mechanisms. And many of them are relatively small—for sharks! Nurse sharks have specially adapted crushing teeth for feeding on hard-shelled animals such as snails, lobsters, crabs, and

sea urchins. Like many specialists, however, they will also eat fishes! They have the capability of rapidly sucking in water and can inhale a fish right into the grinding mechanism. I have seen nurse sharks kept successfully with triggerfishes and moray eels; however, the people who have the most fun with them are those who keep a couple of them in a tank by themselves (or even one, which might be better). These people make virtual pets out of their sharks and entertain visitors by hand feeding them. They even invite guests who want to feed them, too. That way, they can always tell people that they have hand fed sharks—and not be lying. (They will take feeder goldfish or bits of clam or fish from your

hand. They are not picky eaters.) Even nurse sharks eventually get too big for the home aquarium, reaching nearly eight feet in length. Two of the smallest species of bamboo sharks (family Hemiscylidae) are *Hemiscyllium ocellatum* and *Hemiscyllium trispeculare*, which "only" get to be three feet long. Fortunately, sharks are slow growing, so many people are able to

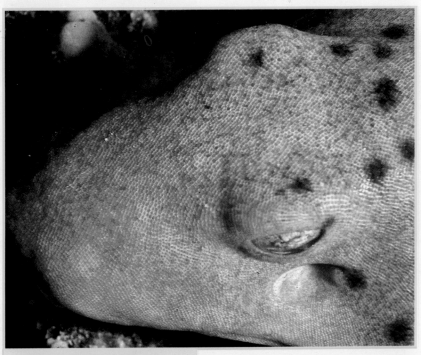

One of the bamboo sharks that is kept in hobbyist's tanks is Hemiscyllium ocellatum. *Photo by Jean Deas.*

keep their pets for many years before taking them to a public aquarium.

Horn Sharks (Heterodontidae)

Horn sharks occur in tropical waters as well as temperate seas, but they look a little less like sharks "should" look (in the public mind) than nurse sharks. They have a robust appearance and have a spine in front of each of the dorsal fins that may be mildly venomous, so these sharks should be handled with caution. As might be surmised from the robust body, the horn sharks are not active swimmers, and, in fact, spend most of their time on the bottom and like a cave made of coral or rock for a hiding place. They will eat live goldfish, chopped clam, shrimp, crab, and any small fishes you have in their tank!

SKATES AND RAYS (ORDER: RAJIFORMES)

Several features set the skates and rays apart from the other elasmobranchs. The greatly enlarged pectoral fins are attached to the sides of the head, and the gills are on the underside of these fins. If the bottom-dwelling skates or rays were to respire normally, all of the bottom mud and detritus would tend to block the flow of water over the gill filaments. To avoid this, these forms have changed their method of respiration, bringing the water in through spiracles on top of the head and then out through the gill chambers.

These are animals that are also not really suited for the home aquarium. The electric rays and the stingrays are even dangerous, and, besides, the electric ray has to be force-fed in captivity. A sting from a stingray is not worth chancing. Such a wound is extremely painful and can even be fatal. Some dealers have the collectors cut off the stinger, which makes them safer as aquarium exhibits. The spine is only used in self defense, but that is of little consolation to waders and swimmers who happen to get stung—or to the hobbyist who gets careless.

There is a certain allure and grace to these animals, and aquarium shops occasionally have them for sale. The prudent aquarist should be sure to get the stingray without the stinger or get a skate that doesn't have the capability of stinging. They will eat shrimp, squid, and chopped clam, among other foods.

BONY FISHES (OSTEICHTHYES)

Lizardfishes (Synodontidae)

The lizardfishes appeal to those aquarists who like to keep "monster" fishes. They not only look like reptiles, they also

Lizardfishes appeal mostly to those aquarists who want a "monster" in their tank. This is Synodus variegatus. *Photo by Roger Steene.*

act like them. Most of their time is spent sitting on the bottom with the body at a slight angle, propped up on the front end by their ventral fins like a jet fighter ready to take off. As soon as a small fish swims by, the lizardfish darts upward with great speed, usually swallowing the prey in

one gulp. The numerous pointed teeth in both jaws, together with the teeth on their tongue, prevent even the most agile fishes from escaping. In captivity, lizardfishes are hardy, but they must have live fishes to eat. Two feedings a week will suffice. About three dozen species of lizardfishes are recognized, and they are a tropical group, but some species migrate north into temperate waters during the summer. All exhibit the characteristic cylindrical shape and reptile-like head. Most of the species have a small adipose fin on the back between the dorsal and tail fins.

Toadfishes (Batrachoididae)

The toadfishes fall into the "monster fish" category, being quite ugly and predaceous. Nonetheless, they are occasionally offered by aquarium shops because they are hardy and have been bred in captivity. Toadfishes are bottom dwelling shallow water fishes that sit on a soft substrate waiting for prey. They have long sharp teeth and have been heard to

Top:Toadfishes also fall into the "monster" category. One that is commonly available is Batrachomoes trispinosus. *Photo by Aaron Norman.*

make a croaking noise. Their appearance and the croaking made the common name inevitable. Some species have venomous spines. Males guard the eggs during the breeding season in a territory that he has staked out. That usually consists of some sort of cave—even a tin can. A toadfish was reported in the aquarium literature to have guarded eggs in a large seashell.

Anglerfishes and Frogfishes (Order: Lophiiformes)

Lophiiform fishes, of which only relatively few species in the about 18 families are known to aquarists, are generally deep water forms. The fishes treated here also have a lure which they use to angle for their prey, but they are generally referred to as frogfishes (Antennariidae). Again, the attraction is more of the monster fish variety but with a bit of humor added.

Bottom: Histrio histrio can amuse visitors for hours as it stalks its prey and suddenly engulfs it with its huge mouth. Photo by Dr. Herbert R. Axelrod.

One of the most popular of the frogfishes among aquarists is *Histrio histrio*, which can amuse visitors by the hour as it "goes fishing," using its lure to attract fellow fishes. These guys are capable of swallowing fishes nearly as big as themselves, even their brothers and sisters so to speak, so you can see why they are not good candidates for the typical community tank.

Catfishes (Suborder Siluroidei)

The last things you might think of in a marine tank are catfishes. The main reason for including them here is to inform hobbyists who do not know otherwise that there are marine catfish families. They are occasionally seen in aquarium shops, but they have not been popular with hobbyists—in direct contrast to the freshwater aquarists.

Sea Catfishes (Ariidae)

These catfishes are tropical and subtropical and have a world-wide distribution. Unlike many of the freshwater catfishes, they are always on the move, often in schools. Of particular interest is that some species, about 40 at least, are mouthbrooders, with the male incubating large eggs the size of marbles. This is of special interest because brood care is rare in marine fishes, as the most expedient method of reproduction, seemingly,

A small school of **Plotosus lineatus.** *This marine catfish is called the "bumble bee" because it packs quite a sting. Photo by Dr. Herbert R. Axelrod.*

is to disperse pelagic eggs, by the thousands, into the plankton. In one species, *Galeichthys felis*, the female develops a special structure on the ventral fins during the breeding season. In spite of this, the male still ends up brooding the eggs!

Catfishes are very rare in marine aquaria. A few, such as this **Arius jordani,** *may be found in marine, brackish, or freshwater aquaria. Photo by Glen S. Axelrod.*

The cleaned skull of an ariid catfish viewed from the underside often has the appearance of a crucifix. In the West Indies and along the coasts of South America these skulls are often sold to gullible tourists as religious objects of sacred value.

Eeltail Catfishes (Plotosidae)

Although there are two dozen species in this family, the one most kept, *Plotosus lineatus*, is also the most dangerous, as it has poisonous spines that can be fatal to certain people. Since the fish is quite active and usually kept in groups, the possibility of being "spined" while netting out a fish or cleaning the tank is far from remote. It has received the common name of "bumblebee catfish" because it is very busy and is able to sting! Although *Plotosus lineatus* lives on the reefs in the Indo-Pacific and is quite colorful when young, it has never been very popular with the marine aquarist. Since some of the species reach 30 inches in length, that is part of the reason why these fishes are not kept, even though the "bumblebee" attains a length of "only" 10 to 12 inches.

Tube-snouted Fishes (Syngnathiformes)

The seven families of this group includes pipefishes and seahorses, which, of course, are popular with aquarists, as well as the trumpet, cornet, snipe, and shrimpfishes. (The rare freshwater Paradox fish from Asia, once included in

A seahorse relative from Australia is the weedy sea dragon (Phyllopteryx taeniolatus). *It grows to about 45 cm. Photo by Dr. Gerald R. Allen.*

A close-up of the head of a seahorse, possibly Hippocampus hippocampus. *The small pectoral fins look almost like "ears." Photo by M. P. & C. Piednoir.*

this group, is now given its own order, Indostomiformes). The members of this order are known not only for their bizarre appearance but also for their strange anatomical and biological characteristics. One feature they all have in common is a long, tubelike snout. Because of this elongated snout, they have all become adept at "sucking in" or pipetting their food. A fast intake of water ensnares a fish in the case of the trumpetfish or tiny member of the plankton for the seahorse. The theme of an armor-plated body and the male incubating the eggs is played out among many families throughout the suborder.

Seahorses and Pipefishes (Syngnathidae)

There are approximately two dozen species of seahorses, many of which are quite popular with hobbyists. All of the seahorses are in the genus *Hippocampus*, which is Latin for "horse caterpillar." Seahorses must be kept by themselves, as other species will outcompete them for food. In nature, they cling to grass or sargassum weed with their prehensile tails and feed upon drifting plankton. In captivity, they can be fed newly-

hatched brine shrimp, and this is a perfect food even for the adults, as it is extremely nutritious (if fed before the first molt), and it won't carry diseases (since you hatched it from cysts or eggs).

Although seahorses don't provide much in the way of

Pipefishes, like this Doryrhamphus excisus, *can be quite colorful and are welcome additions to a marine aquarium, but they cannot be kept with aggressive fishes. Photo by K.-H. Choo.*

three anal spines are the identifying features of the family. Many of the species are mouthbrooders, and many have been bred in captivity. In some species the male incubates the eggs and in others the female takes care of that chore. Since the cardinals are sometimes amazingly abundant in a particular locality, they must play an important role in the food cycles of larger carnivorous forms. Although most cardinalfishes are relatively shallow water fishes, there are deep water forms complete with luminescent organs. The family is circumtropical, with some species even entering fresh water as long as there aren't any freshwater competitors already present.

Although species of this family would be considered colorful in freshwater aquaria, they often are not flashy enough for marine hobbyists. Because they have a unique appearance, are hardy, are a nice size for aquaria, and have, in fact, bred in aquaria, the marine cardinals are included here. It is interesting to note that the freshwater cardinal tetra, *Cheirodon axelrodi*, which of course are not related to the marine cardinals even remotely, are actually more colorful than their marine namesakes.

The cardinals are nocturnal, and they are not likely to be seen by divers in the daylight hours unless they look in dark areas of the reef for them.

Snappers (Lutjanidae)

Snappers are certainly not for the "normal" community tank, as they are efficient predators and cannot be trusted with fishes large enough for them to swallow. They *can* be included in a community tank of unusual fishes, such as a moray eel, a triggerfish, a squirrelfish, and a large angelfish. They also are good candidates for tanks that have a single fish that is kept

The barbels of the goatfish are used for probing sandy bottoms for invertebrates that live just under the surface. Photo of Upeneichthys lineatus *by Dr. Gerald R. Allen.*

because of its interesting behavior or pet-like qualities. The schoolmaster snappers or emperor snappers are good candidates for "pets" if kept by themselves. Snappers are difficult to describe, and yet they are easy to identify by their "snapper appearance." This consists of a generalized fish shape, sharp canine teeth, and a long and flattened snout profile.

In nature, snappers are usually shallow-water species that prey upon fishes and, opportunistically, on other animals as well. They generally travel in schools, but some species are less inclined to school than others and solitary individuals of all species can be found. These are very characteristic fishes, in terms of numbers, of the coral reef. For some reason not clearly understood, the family is not represented in Hawaii, although there have been

With its extraordinary fin development, Symphorichthys spilurus *is one of the more spectacular snappers. Photo by U. Erich Friese.*

Platax batavianus, *like other members of the genus, is quite attractive when small but with growth becomes less colorful. Photo by Klaus Paysan.*

A lone Heniochus acuminatus *in its natural habitat. Some people call it the "poor man's Moorish idol." Photo by Cathy Church.*

ever, all the species get a little large for most aquaria, and they are not ideal scavengers anyway. The fact is that they can be a challenge to keep, and they should only be kept for their own interest. That is not to say that they won't perform useful functions in the aquarium, such as keeping the gravel worked over and helping to prevent any dead spots in which the water is not flowing properly.

Although species of goatfishes are often available in aquarium shops, they should not be bought on an impulse. These fishes are quite sensitive to water quality and need at least three feedings a day of a varied and nutritious diet.

Spadefishes and Batfishes (Ephippidae)

The juvenile batfishes are either adored or hated by

Forcipiger flavissimus *can reach food items that have fallen into crevices with its elongate snout. Photo by Dr. Herbert R. Axelrod.*

several attempts to get them started there as a possible food fish.

Goatfishes (Mullidae)

The goatfishes have two long, tactile barbels under the chin that constantly probe the bottom as though looking for land mines. What they are really seeking are invertebrates that live in the sand, but they will also scavenge. They are often thought of by the hobbyist as a scavenger for the marine tank. How-

marine hobbyists. There does not seem to be an intermediate position. While undoubtedly colorful and stately, some hobbyists don't feel that they measure up in terms of color to other coral reef fishes. Although delicate in appearance, these fishes are   actually quite hardy and good feeders. The main problem with them is that they can reach a large size, and the adult form is not nearly as charming as their juveniles. All the faults are outweighed in the eyes of many hobbyists by the charms of the

Heniochus acuminatus *does well in captivity. It is often called the banner fish because of the long dorsal spine. Photo by Ken Lucas, Steinhart Aquarium.*

juvenile. Not only is it regal in bearing and appearance, but it responds to the aquarist in an almost pet-like manner, and it quickly learns to take food from the fingers which proffer it.

Butterflyfishes (Chaetodontidae)

Butterflyfishes are among the most beautiful fishes on the coral reef, and many species are found as mated pairs. These fishes don't defend their eggs or larvae, so there has been much speculation as to why they occur in pairs. The main line of thought is that it assures the male of a mate during spawning, and the female benefits because the male does most of the defending of the foraging range, so she gets to feed more. In any case, it is difficult to keep more than one individual of a species in a tank unless you get a mated pair that was captured in the wild.

Butterflyfishes are definitely in the difficult category, and some species are impossible to keep because of extremely specialized feeding behavior. One of the most dramatic species that does well in the aquarium is *Forcipiger flavissimus*. This species comes to the surface and squirts water out its long snout frequently enough that early ichthyologists were tempted to place it with the archerfishes. The snout is used in the wild to reach into deep recesses, and the ability to blow water probably helps stir up prey crustaceans.

The *Forcipiger* are quite aggressive with each other in the aquarium, so only one should be kept in a tank. These fish have an unusual method of attack, utilizing their dorsal fin spines. These spines are erected as *Forcipiger* turns at an angle in order to attack the other fish with them. These fishes will even fight in plastic bags when they are collected and must be bagged individually or shipped with different species.

Generally, butterflyfishes are not so quarrelsome, and there are many beautiful species from which to choose. The question is their suitability for aquarium life rather than their aggressiveness.

The banner butterflyfish, *Heniochus acuminatus*, is similar in appearance to the Moorish idol, and is often called the "poor man's Moorish idol," but it is much more hardy, and it is consequently popular with hobbyists.

Marine Angelfishes (Pomacanthidae)

With just a few exceptions, the angels are among the most beautiful fishes on Earth. In fact, they are certainly among the most

Heniochus acuminatus *sampling the invertebrates on the reef. Because it is a nibbler it is not recommended for a reef tank. Photo by Cathy Church.*

A young Chaetodon trifascialis *flitting around the branches of an* Acropora *coral. Photo by Roger Steene.*

Chaetodon trifasciatus *is one of those butterflyfishes that need a special diet for it to survive. It may survive in some reef tanks but will feed on the invertebrates there. Photo by Ken Lucas, Steinhart Aquarium.*

The flame-back pygmy angelfish (Centropyge aurantonotus) remains small and does well in captivity. Photo by Aaron Norman.

Holacanthus tricolor *feeds primarily on sponges in its natural habitat and is difficult to feed in captivity. It undergoes less of a color change with age than some other large angelfishes. Photo by Klaus Paysan.*

beautiful *animals* on Earth. The problem is that some species grow to a length of two feet—a little large for the average aquarium. Fortunately, they do have a protracted juvenile stage. Also, there are "pygmy angels," but many of them are not quite as hardy as their larger brethren.

It is interesting to note that the butterflyfishes generally have very similar coloration as juveniles, but almost without exception, the angels have radically different juvenile coloration. This has been both a puzzlement and consternation to ichthyologists. It caused earlier systematists to classify juveniles and adults in separate species, and ethologists have been at a loss as to why the coloration should be different. One idea is that the difference in coloration makes for more toleration by adult conspecifics, allowing the young ones to remain in the territory of the adults until they are capable of surviving on their own, but laboratory testing has so far not supported this speculation.

Angels can easily be distinguished from butterflyfishes by the presence of a strong spine on their preoperculum.

Only a few species live as mated pairs, as is the case with most butterflyfishes. Most live in complex harem-like groups, with one male dominating over a very large reef area that comprises the territories of a number of

The bright yellow lemonpeel pigmy angelfish (Centropyge flavissimus) is very popular with marine aquarists. Photo by Karl Knaack.

Holacanthus passer from the tropical eastern Pacific has been called the king angelfish. It has a "crown" similar to that sported by the queen angel from the Caribbean. Photo by Dr. Herbert R. Axelrod.

An Amphiprion ocellaris *snuggles in the protective stinging tentacles of an anemone. Photo by Roger Steene.*

This Amphiprion ocellaris *looks kind of lost without an anemone. Photo by John Manzione.*

mon" anemonefish, *Amphiprion ocellaris,* and most of the other species of the genus are quite colorful, too. The maroon clownfish,

The maroon clownfish (Premnas aculeatus) is in a genus all its own but behaves pretty much like other anemonefishes. Photo by Dr. Herbert R. Axelrod.

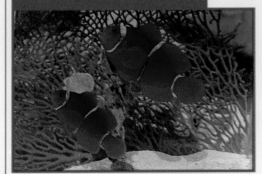

Premmas biaculeatus, is in a genus all of its own, but it, too, is quite beautiful and a hardy aquarium fish. This species can be kept in pairs in home or office aquaria, and they will spawn in the tank, too. In fact, clownfishes have been spawned commercially more than any other marine species, and tank-raised fry are often available and are the preferred purchase by knowledgeable aquarists.

To add to their appeal, the damselfishes also have in their family a number of "blue devils" (several species of several genera) which perfectly compliment the color of the clownfishes. In fact, a clownfish and a blue devil are breathtaking all by themselves in a tank. And that is before adding the angels, butterflyfishes, and tangs.

To be sure, the rose has its thorns, and damselfishes have their dark side, too, for aquarists. Nearly all of them are quite aggressive. Even clownfishes, which are considered mild for damsels, will attack fishes much bigger than themselves while defending their anemone. And other species of damsels are similar in their territorial behavior. Nevertheless, this is a very desirable family, the members being for the most part hardy and

Chrysiptera parasema *is one of the many solid blue colored damselfishes often referred to as blue devils. Photo by Aaron Norman.*

The blue and yellow colors inspired the describer to name this fish Chrysiptera hemicyanea, *the species name meaning half blue. Photo by Dr. Gerald R. Allen.*

*The beaubrummel (*Stegastes flavilatus*) is omnivorous, foraging on invertebrates but it may take some benthic algae as well. Photo by Alex Kerstitch.*

Species of the genus Dascyllus *are hardy, inexpensive, and very popular. One of the commonly offered species is D. trimaculatus. Photo by Andre Roth.*

hawkfish, *Oxycirrhitus typus.*

Wrasses (Labridae)

There is a tremendous variation in size among the approximately 600 species of wrasses, almost all of which are carnivorous. They range from the tiny 3-inch pencil-like species of the genus *Labroides* to the giants of the genus *Cheilinus*, measuring ten feet and weighing several hundred pounds. Many are highly colored, and they are among the most brilliantly

The sling-jawed wrasse (Epibulus insidiator) has a lower jaw that can be extended far forward. Photo by Klaus Paysan.

colored of the common coral reef fishes. As with the angels and so many marine fish species, the juvenile forms and colors are usually dramatically different from the adult. And some species have an intermediate color phase, too.

Wrasses are usually non-schooling fishes that swim primarily via the action of their pectoral fins. They are noted for their well-developed incisor or canine teeth. Many of them use these

Bird wrasses are good candidates for a community tank. Photo of Gomphosus varius *by Dr. Herbert R. Axelrod.*

teeth to advantage against conspecifics as well as other fishes in the aquarium. Selection of species must be done cautiously here for the community tank.

One of the remarkable things about wrasses is that they have developed the trait of sleeping under the sand. This is probably a defense

Good species for the community tank are the cleaner wrasses of the genus Labroides. *They will actually pick parasites and dead skin off of other fishes. Photo of* Labroides pectoralis *by Dr. Walter A. Starck II.*

against moray eels, which prowl the waters at night looking for sleeping fishes. What may seem like an empty tank can soon be filled with swimming wrasses shortly after the light is switched on.

A peculiar species is the long-jawed wrasse, *Epibulus insidiator*, which has a lower jaw that is about twice the usual length and can be extended forward for an even greater distance. This

Gomphosus caeruleus is another bird wrasse. The elongated snout allows it to poke into cracks and crevices to obtain food that other, short-snouted fishes cannot reach. This adaptation is not limited to the wrasses but appears in many other, completely unrelated fishes. Photo by Roger Steene.

The teeth of parrotfishes are fused to form a "beak" as can be clearly seen in this close-up of the beak of Scarus guacamaia. *Photo by Dr. Walter A. Starck II.*

obviously is not a species for the community tank, as it can snatch up tank mates that mistakenly feel that they are a safe distance away. Good species for the community tank are the small *Labroides* species or one of the bird wrasses of the genus *Gomphosus*.

Parrotfishes (Scaridae)
These species swim in

Young parrotfishes sometimes find their way into marine aquaria, especially if they are colorful ones like this Cetoscarus bicolor. *Photo by Dr. Herbert R. Axelrod.*

the same manner as the wrasses, and they are often quite colorful, too. They are not generally good specimens for the community tank for two reasons. The first is that almost all the species get quite large. The second is that members of this family do not generally do well in captivity. One reason is that on the reef they feed by using their powerful beaks and strong pharyngeal teeth to grind up the coral "houses" and digest the corals inside. (A lot of the gleaming white coral sand on tropical beaches is there courtesy of the parrotfishes!) The feeding problem can be partly alleviated by feeding vacation blocks, and the parrotfishes will take some food, but there is no denying that they are a challenge to keep. Only dedicated parrotfish lovers should even try one of these fishes.

Jawfishes (Opistognathidae)
The jawfishes are a small tropical group of secretive fishes, some of which live in burrows of their own construction.

*The most popular jawfish with marine aquarists is the yellow head jawfish (*Opistognathus aurifrons*).*

All members of the family have large mouths, and a few have long, backward extensions of the jaw-bones that enables the tremendous mouth to open even wider. This enables the fish to scoop up food in the water column, much like a pelican uses its bill as a net.

Jawfishes are so named because of their large mouths. They are mouthbrooders, the males taking over the incubating chores. Photo of Opistognathus *sp. by Dr. Patrick L. Colin.*

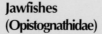

These fishes are considered good for the living reef aquarium since they feed from the water column and are not likely to browse on invertebrates.

A pair of jawfish in the aquarium can be real clowns. They dig a tunnel

Ecsenius tigris *in its natural habitat on a coral reef. Blennies are comical little fishes that do well in both fish-only and reef tanks. Photo by Roger Steene.*

into which they retreat at any sign of danger. They decorate the entrance to their dwelling with little rocks and will steal the rocks from the entrance of the neighboring jawfish, and many harmless fights will ensue, consisting almost entirely of bluff.

Three different species of blennies are coexisting in this marine aquarium. The one most sought after by marine aquarists is of course the red one, Lipophrys nigriceps. Photo by Karl Knaack.

Blennies (Blenniidae)

Actually, there are several families of blennies in the suborder Blennioidei, but the combtooth blennies are the ones that aquarists usually keep. Even these specimens can cause problems in the aquarium, as they are often territorial and therefore quarrelsome with other fishes. They should be carefully selected for the typical community tank. The truth is, blennies are not outrageously colorful, but they are unique and are loaded with personality. Once again, we have species that might best be kept by themselves as pets or in a very specialized community tank. Even though they tend to be territorial, especially during breeding season, it is possible to have a blenny community tank, with lots of rocks and caves.

Blennies are one of the types of fishes that have

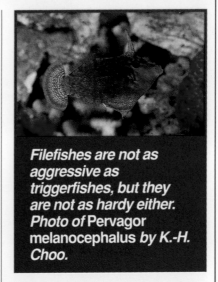

Filefishes are not as aggressive as triggerfishes, but they are not as hardy either. Photo of Pervagor melanocephalus *by K.-H. Choo.*

greatly reduced swim bladders in order to fight the currents and hop around from rock to coral to rock. They are smart little fishes and learn every inch of the tank with all the nooks and crannies. They are gluttonous eaters and quickly learn to take food from the aquarist's hands—even if they must tread water while doing so. They are quite

Ecsenius fijiensis *as the name implies comes from the Fiji Islands. Almost any of the species of* Ecsenius *make good aquarium pets. Photo by Dr. Bruce Carlson.*

Ecsenius axelrodi was named to honor Dr. Herbert R. Axelrod. It comes in a variety of different color patterns. Photos by Roger Steene.

hardy, being about as "bullet proof" as marine fishes come.

Triggerfishes and Filefishes (Family Balistidae)

There has been a trend recently to unite the former families Balistidae (triggerfishes) and Monacanthidae (filefishes) into one family.

Rhinecanthus rectangulus *is commonly seen in marine aquaria. But beware, triggers have powerful jaws and can do a lot of damage to other fishes. Photo by Karl Frogner.*

The Ostraciontidae (boxfishes) and various puffers have been included with this family under the Order Plectognathi. In actual practice, marine hobbyists have always recognized that there is great similarity in triggerfishes and filefishes, but there are great differences, too. For one thing, triggerfishes are tough guys. They are hardy and resistant to diseases in aquaria. But

they have powerful jaws, and they can wreak havoc among other fishes. This is not because they are extremely aggressive, as is the case with many damsels. It is just that they have such powerful jaws that they can cause such damage when they do act aggressively.

Part of the problem with triggerfishes is that they are highly evolved nibblers, with the absurdly small yet extremely powerful mouth. Triggers thus tend to nibble at everything in a curious sort of way, and that includes the coral, any plants, and fellow tank mates—just out of curiosity, of course, but they still do considerable damage. In nature, not so much aggression is seen, as the other fishes are not hemmed in by a tank so that they cannot escape the inquisitive jaws of the triggerfishes. Nevertheless, at least some species of triggerfish do establish territories in nature, and many species live in harems. One male presides over perhaps an entire patch reef which encompasses the territories of several females. The male cruises the entire reef,

helping to defend all the territories, while the females each defend their own section of the reef. Not all fishes are driven away, but certainly other triggers of the same species are. Since triggers feed primarily on crustaceans, other fishes with similar diets are more likely to be excluded.

When spawning time arrives, the female digs a depression and lays large grape-like eggs, which she defends after they have been fertilized by the male. Instead of fanning the eggs to keep them oxygenated and free of debris, the female blows water over the eggs. Divers must be wary during such times, as guarding female triggers will attack them and bite them viciously with their powerful little mouths. One of the Cousteau movies ("World without Sun") showed a diver being attacked by a guarding female, and the diver had prepared for the event by putting extra padding

Another favorite triggerfish with marine aquarists is Rhinecanthus aculeatus. Photo by Ken Lucas, Steinhart Aquarium.

under his wet suit. Cousteau also mentioned having seen guarding triggerfishes chasing off even sharks in their zeal to protect their eggs.

With such large territories, it can be imagined that it would be difficult to induce triggerfishes to get along, let alone spawn, in the aquarium. Yet, spawnings of some species have taken place. Unfortu-

The most sought after triggerfish is the clown trigger (Balistoides conspicillum). Young clown triggerfishes are exceptionally difficult to find. Photo by Dr. Herbert R. Axelrod.

nately, I know of no instance in which the young have been raised. While it is true that the triggerfishes seem to have a prolonged planktonic larval form, it must be admitted that species of

triggerfish have not been targeted for large-scale spawning attempts. They are, at best, a marginal species for community tanks, so their popularity has its limits. Having said that, I must confess to a special fondness for triggerfishes myself. And the triggerfishes are a group that has maintained a small but consistent following. They make great display specimens when kept alone, and they can be kept in very specialized community fish tanks that consist of rough and tough fishes.

Many filefish species, however, are good candidates for the community tank. They are not as hardy as triggerfishes, but they aren't as formidable nor as aggressive either. Filefishes differ from triggerfishes in having the spine further forward, and they have longer, slimmer

bodies. Filefishes tend to feed more from the water column, and they are more finicky eaters than their triggerfish brethren.

The fact is that triggerfishes have a number of methods of predation and are fun to watch. They will prey upon crabs or sea urchins, either of which is well armed. The crabs often are concealed below the sand. Triggerfish specimens will browse along the bottom and blow at the sand, thus exposing the crabs, which might not be seen if their "unearthing" didn't immediately activate their defensive, threatening mode. The powerful jaws of the triggerfishes make short work of the carapace of the crab. The triggerfishes have numerous ways of attacking a sea urchin. One is to simply pick it up by the spines and drop it, trying to get to the underbelly where the spines are shorter. Alternatively, it may systematically simply bite off the spines, one by one, until it can get to the carapace of the echinoderm. Finally, it may approach the sea urchin by blowing a trench through the sand in order to get underneath it. All of this gives only a hint of the intricacies of the triggerfish species and helps explain the appeal that they have had for marine hobbyists, in spite of the fact that they are so troublesome!

A yellow puffer,
Arothron meleagris,
being cleaned by a
cleaner wrasse
Labroides dimidiatus.
Photo by Klaus Paysan.

Puffers and Boxfishes (Several Families)

Again, these are not species that are suitable for typical community tanks. One of the problems with boxfishes is that some exude toxic compounds, especially when frightened, and they scare easily. Once acclimated, the danger seems slight, but it is ever present nonetheless. One of the displays that many hobbyists want to set up is one of cowfishes (certain species of boxfish) with sea horses. This can, in fact, be done successfully, as cowfishes will not outcompete the sea horses for food. And what a display it makes, with some of the fishes looking like horses and the others looking like sea going cows!

Puffers are quite hardy, but they have some of the problems of triggerfishes, in that some species are quite aggressive and they have the same powerful jaws that characterize triggerfishes. Many species are quite peaceful, nearly shy, and some have an amusing appearance, looking for all the world like a potato. The diodontidids (porcupinefish) have a particular appeal and make great pets in a tank by themselves. They also have powerful jaws that can be used on tank mates, but their unusual appearance helps earn them their own tank. Their winning personality can also earn them their own tank, as they are very responsive to their keepers and love to take food from your fingers. Just be careful they don't get your fingers. Those jaws really are powerful!

Many hobbyists want to set up a display of cowfishes and seahorses. One of the most popular cowfishes is Lactoria cornutus. *Photo by Klaus Paysan.*

Porcupinefishes can swallow water (or air) until their bodies have swollen up almost into a balloon. The spines sticking out will deter most predators. Photo by Cathy Church of Diodon hystrix.

SUGGESTED READING

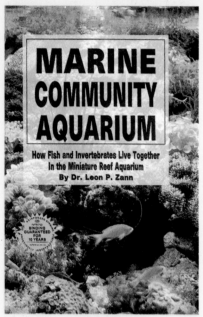

H-1101

Hard cover, 5.5 x 8.5 in., 416 pages, 315 full color photos, 83 black and white photos, 33 drawings. Deals with symbiotic relationships.

H-1103

Hard cover, 8.5 x 11 in., 192 pages, 315 full color photos, many line drawings. A scientifically based guide for the beginner and advanced hobbyist alike.

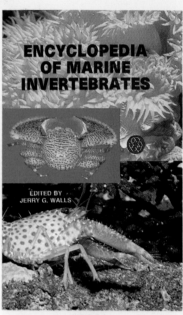

H-951

Hard cover, 5.5 x 8 in., 736 pages. Over 600 full-color photos, many line drawings. Written by a panel of experts this book is a superb compilation of information on the invertebrates.

PS-735

Hard cover, 8.5 x 11 in., 208 pages. 191 color photos and 99 black and white photos. A basic book covering setting up a marine tank, keeping it running, and keeping fishes healthy.

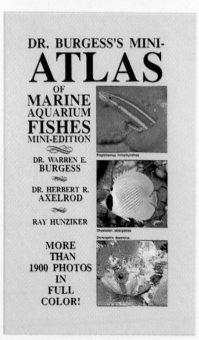

H-1107

Hard cover, 5.5 x 8.5 in., almost 1,000 pages, and almost 2,000 color photos. A combination of explanations of every aspect of setting up and maintaining a marine aquarium and an atlas of fish photos for identification purposes.

TS-133

Hard cover, 8.25 x 11 in., 208 pages. More than 600 full-color photos and drawings. A highly practical and highly useful approach to the saltwater aquarium.

INDEX

Page numbers in **boldface** refer to illustrations.